An opinionated guide to

LISBON

Written by
RUBY CONWAY

INFORMATION IS DEAD. LONG LIVE OPINION.

When we conceived these guidebooks, we feared they would fail. Who needs a guidebook when everything can be found online for free?

But then it occurred to us: that's exactly why you *do* want a guidebook. You want lively, trustworthy opinion combined with great photographs. You don't want endless information from a thousand online bots.

We think you are like us: you care about quality, you care about style, you care about provenance, but you don't have time to waste on long words like 'provenance'. You want to cut to the chase: where's good?

We are an independent from London. How dare we write a book about Lisbon? Because we work with passionate local writers who seek out the spots that remind us of the east London we know and love: these are the most creative, diverse and exciting places of all.

Ann & Martin, co-founders
Hoxton Mini Press

BAR DE VINHOS
Pratinhos

Insaciável (no.77)

Basílica da Estrela (no. 50)
Opposite: Pátio do Tijolo (no. 72)

Canalha (no.6)

Opposite: Fonte da Telha (no.68)

CITY OF LIGHT

It's rare to find a cosmopolitan city as in rhythm with the elements as Lisbon, moving as it does to the pulse of sun and tide. Surfboards and parasols are frequently sighted on metros and trains, locals making their regular escape to the wild Atlantic. This is a city of gathering outside – a mass exodus to rugged sandy beaches (no.69, no.70) by day and a return to *miradouros* (viewpoints), *praças* (squares) and cobbled streets by evening. Come dusk, the light in Lisbon aches, amber rippling across its hills and onto the River Tejo. It is said that being able to look out over wide-open vistas to the horizon is a balm for the spirit, and Lisbon has this effect, with its sweeping views of water, cliffs and the inky-blue outlines of the Serra da Arrábida mountains. Of course, life beats on, but looking upon this landscape brings with it currents of calm, the edges somehow smoothed over.

Perhaps it is this proximity to nature that invokes Lisbon's easy-going spirit and slower pace. People don't like to plan ahead here; they follow the mood of the day as it comes. There's an unpredictability to the hours, to where a day or night might take you and who you might meet along the way.

And this is a polyphonic city, carrying a chorus of languages and cultures. It's easy to stumble upon an unexpected cultural gathering, where the spirit of dance and music brings out a different attitude to life – between Portuguese street parties heady with smoking sardines during Santos Populares (popular saints' festivals), Samba on street corners, Brazilian carnival and pulsing Afrobeats parties. With mass immigration from the Portuguese-speaking world – Brazil, Angola, Mozambique, Cape Verde, to name a few – as well as South Asia and wider Europe, the city is truly culturally diverse. This is also affirmed by its rich and varied culinary offerings: spiced Nepalese momo dumplings, infamous clandestine Chinese restaurants, hot-out-the-oven Brazilian pão de queijo (baked cheese balls) and Angolan Moamba de Galina (rich chicken stew).

While Lisbon has always been shaped by movement – the coming and going of people – the last few years have seen tidal shifts, with longing calls to protect the local culture. Still so much of the city's charm lies in what remains unchanged, those places that are pure tradition. There's nothing quite like the feel of a *tasca* (no.10, no.31) – a no-frills Portuguese eatery, often long-standing and family-run, where regulars greet owners and waiters by name. It's no-surprises fare at good prices, silver platters of the grilled catch-of-the-day, big pots of seafood rice and bitoque (egg-topped steak) slapped down on paper tablecloths, where the hours feel long and full. Then there's the grand old *pastelarias* (no.29) that belong to a different era, sugary, custard-heady Bolas de Berlim buns carted around beaches to the chant of a solitary salesperson, and espressos drunk at countertops. Of course, with the buzzy onslaught of coffee shops and small plates restaurants set against the traditional, older establishments, we find ourselves in an increasingly divided city. A pervasive modern tale.

Nostalgia is supposedly endemic to the Portuguese condition, so perhaps it is inevitable to feel the longing for the past that Lisbon invokes across its spirited and soulful locales. Some of the greatest writings on the city – from Pessoa, Saramego, Tabucchi – speak to a place that sits somewhere between dream and waking, layered with ghosts, memories and history. And between crumbling palaces, grand statues and chipped tiles, weathering under the weight of the past, it's impossible not to feel it.

Ruby Conway
Lisbon, 2026

Ruby Conway is a culture and lifestyle writer and editor whose work has been published in *The Sunday Times*, *Dazed*, *The Face*, *Wallpaper**, *Huck*, *AnOther* and *Service95*. She currently lives in Lisbon, uncovering the local culture scene, exploring the coast and looking for the best chocolate mousse in the city. She can be found on Instagram at @passtherubicon.

HOW TO NAVIGATE
THE CITY

If your legs are up to the challenge of its steep hills and narrow cobbled streets, Lisbon is a city which deserves to be walked. Its streets are for drifting through; its regular *miradouros* for expansive cityscape views. If not, outside the older parts of the city, the metro system (complete with tile artwork) is by far the easiest way to get around. City bikes are also on hand, offering a scenic way to glide along the waterfront.

Then there are the buses, trams, trains and ferries journeying to and fro across the River Tejo. While they're rickety to ride and often full of tourists, Lisbon's classic trams are like something out of a Wes Anderson film, with vintage wooden interiors, leather seats and open windows.

For a taste of the city-beach lifestyle, trains on the picturesque Linha de Cascais run from the city along the coast – the Tejo transitioning into the Atlantic Ocean. You can use one of the city's Navegante cards across all modes of transport.

Bolt or Uber is your best choice for reaching further-flung spots, sometimes in combination with public transport. Ride-hailing is criminally cheap in Lisbon and an alternative way to traverse the city, particularly late at night when public transport stops running.

BEST FOR...

Old-school Lisbon

Lisbon's iconic establishments will transport you to a different time, from the grandeur of Pastelaria Versailles (no.29) to '60s snack bar Galeto (no.25). For a drinking spot, ring to enter the Art-Nouveau A Paródia (no.81) and stock up on timeless Portuguese products at A Vida Portuguesa (no.33).

Portuguese art

Experience two of Portugal's most prominent artists between Casa das Histórias Paula Rego (no.48) and Fundação Arpad Szenes – Vieira da Silva (no.55). Elsewhere, the Centro de Arte Moderna, part of the Gulbenkian Foundation (no.46), holds the country's largest collection of modern art.

Wild coastlines

It's hard to comprehend how close you are to the city on the nature-rich Costa da Caparica, with its expansive sandy beaches of Fonte da Telha (no.68) and Praia da Saúde (no.69). Alternatively, head west to Praia do Guincho (no.70), with its untamed bay and dunes backdropped by the Sintra Mountains.

Portuguese grandeur

Where to start in a city filled with palaces and monuments? The detailing of the Mosteiro dos Jerónimos (no.51) and Palácio Fronteira (no.52) is unmatched. For a Baroque showcase, look to the Panteão Nacional (no.54) and the Águas Livres Aqueduct (no.57). Or book a heritage stay in former convents Santa Clara 1728 (no.71) or Locke de Santa Joana (no.74).

Independent shops

Discover sustainable brands at Fairly Normal (no.42) and Gandaia (no.43), both born in Lisbon. Local designers abound at concept stores EmbaiXada (no.36) and Kintu Studio (no.39), while classic Portuguese products fill the shelves of A Vida Portuguesa (no.33) and Companhia Portugueza do Chá (no.37).

Green escapes

Hide away in Lisbon's tropical pockets in Jardim da Estrela (no.58), Tapada das Necessidades (no.60) and Estufa Fria (no.62). For striking modernist landscaping, explore the bamboo-clad walkways of the Gulbenkian (no.46) Garden.

Sunset vistas

The city is at its best at sunset, and Miradouro do Monte Agudo (no.79), as well as hilltop parks Jardim do Torel (no.61) and Jardim da Cerca da Graça (no.59), deliver views with equally good vibes. Alternatively, catch the ferry to Jardim do Rio (no.63) to watch the sun sink behind the water.

Local sounds

Lisbon is a city of music, with a vibrant nightlife scene. Tejo Bar (no.82) is a cult spot, while at Amor Records (no.80), Fábrica Braço de Prata (no.84) and Duro de Matar (no.16), you'll stumble across diverse sets and genres.

A PERFECT WEEKEND

Friday night

Start with a drink at Amor Records (no.80) before ascending to Monte Agudo (no.79) for another glass as the sun goes down. Amble over to the seafood institution Cervejaria Ramiro (no.24) for a Lisbon ritual, or for something vegetarian-friendly, try Patuá (no.18) for Macanese dishes.

Saturday morning

Hop on a train or tram to Belém and start the day with a pastel de nata from Manteigaria (no.19) before wandering the ornate cloister of Mosteiro dos Jerónimos (no.51). For modern art, the CCB (no.47) is just around the corner, or stroll down the waterfront to modern architecture icon the MAAT (no.45).

Saturday lunch

Continue your Lisbon seafood odyssey with lunch at Último Porto (no.10) – a staple grilled fish spot. Or for elevated Portuguese culinary classics, acclaimed restaurant Canalha (no.6) sits just behind the MAAT (no.45).

Saturday afternoon

After the post-lunch slump, do what Lisboetas do best and drift over to the beach for the afternoon. Catch the train to Praia de São Pedro do Estoril (no.65) or Praia da Azarujinha (no.67) for a dose of sunbathing, swimming and cold beers.

Saturday evening

Back in the city, venture to the post-industrial Marvila district for the evening. Dig into tacos and tunes at Duro de Matar (no.16) or sample the line-up at Fábrica Braço de Prata (no.84).

Sunday morning

Shake off last night's cobwebs with a Brazilian brunch at Uaipi (no.9) before some light shopping. Potter between Salted Books (no.38), tea emporium Companhia Portugueza do Chá (no.37), Kintu Studio (no.39) for artisan pieces and Gandaia (no.43) for fashion.

Sunday lunch

Head to the sun-dappled square Praça das Flores and enjoy some prime people-watching over an ice cream from Nannarella (no.20). For something more substantial, sample Persian plates at Cafeh Tehran (no.13).

Sunday afternoon

Drift over to Jardim da Estrela (no.58) and enjoy a drink at one of its kiosks. Stroll to Jardim das Amoreiras and marvel at the Águas Livres Aqueduct (no.57) or peruse abstract art at the Fundação Arpad Szenes – Vieira da Silva (no.55) gallery.

Sunday evening

Swing by natural wine bar Insaciável (no.77) for an aperitivo. Then, for a final dinner on the town, visit Nordic Familjen (no.7) or Prado (no.26) for its farm-to-table plates.

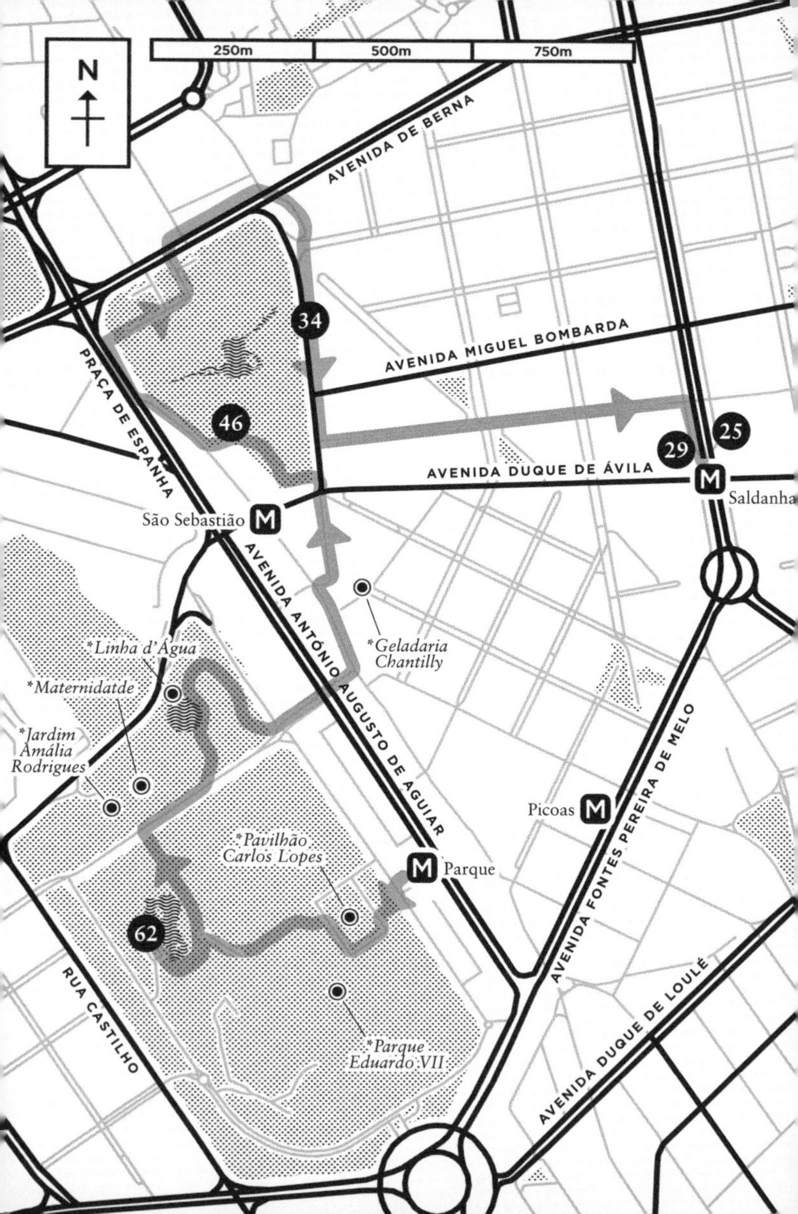

N
250m
500m
750m
AVENIDA DE BERNA
AVENIDA MIGUEL BOMBARDA
AVENIDA DUQUE DE ÁVILA
34
46
29
25
PRAÇA DE ESPANHA
São Sebastião
Saldanha
AVENIDA ANTÓNIO AUGUSTO DE AGUIAR
*Linha d'Água
*Maternidatde
*Jardim
Amália
Rodrigues
*Geladaria
Chantilly
*Pavilhão
Carlos Lopes
Picoas
AVENIDA FONTES PEREIRA DE MELO
Parque
62
RUA CASTILHO
*Parque
Eduardo VII
AVENIDA DUQUE DE LOULÉ

1

WALK: THE MODERN CITY

Standout architecture, landscaping and urban design

From Parque metro station, head towards *Parque Eduardo VII**, climbing up to the pastel-orange *Pavilhão Carlos Lopes** and around to its tiled facade. Stroll across the grand park, with its maze-like hedges, and down to the concealed botanical garden, Estufa Fria ❷; its entrance is marked by a statue-studded lake with geese and peacocks. Post plant-peruse, continue up the park's wide, tree-lined avenue, pausing at the viewpoint at its peak. Pass through the *Jardim Amália Rodrigues**, glimpsing Fernando Botero's bronze sculpture *Maternidade**, before stopping for a drink at *Linha d'Água**, with its sculpted pool. Continue through the Largo de São Sebastião da Pedreira, making a pit stop at *Geladaria Chantilly** for excellent ice cream. Just over at the Gulbenkian Foundation ❹⓺, start your art musings with the Centro de Arte Moderna, before continuing to the Calouste Gulbenkian Museum. Loop around the landscaped gardens before swinging by indie print locale Under the Cover ❸⓸. Turn onto Avenida João Crisóstomo and head to '60s snack bar Galeto ❷⓹ to finish your saunter. Or, for a sweet treat, visit the pastry counter of the grand Versailles ❷⓽ cafe opposite.

Length: 4 km
Walking time without stops: 1 hour
Start: Parque Metro
**Not in guidebook*

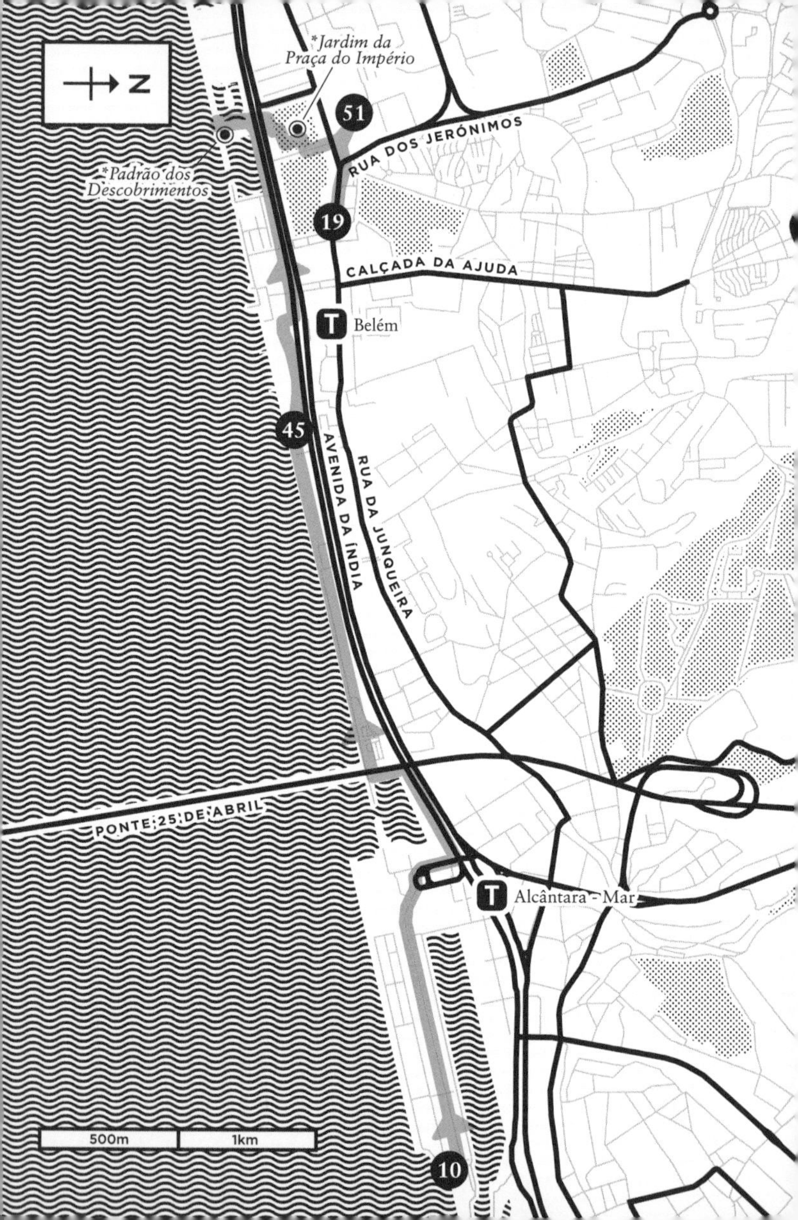
*Jardim da
Praça do Império
51
RUA DOS JERÓNIMOS
*Padrão dos
Descobrimentos
19
CALÇADA DA AJUDA
T Belém
45
AVENIDA DA ÍNDIA
RUA DA JUNQUEIRA
PONTE 25 DE ABRIL
T Alcântara - Mar
500m
1km
10

2

WALK: ALONG THE TEJO

Waterfront sardines and sights

For miraculously flat terrain, amble along Lisbon's marina-studded riverfront walkway, with glorious views of the 25 de Abril suspension bridge towering over the River Tejo. Begin with a grilled-fish lunch on the docks at no-frills Portuguese joint Último Porto **10**. Full-bellied, make your way along the Doca de Alcântara, boats bobbing in the harbour, and under the bridge. On one side, sailboats drift past, on the other, contemporary sculptures signal the approaching modern art gallery the MAAT **45**. Step inside to browse the exhibitions, or walk along its sloping roof to admire the cutting-edge architecture and views. Along with a steady flow of runners and cyclists, press on to the next marina, Doca de Belém, and around to the *Padrão dos Descobrimentos** (Monument to the Discoveries). Pivot away from the water, passing through the *Jardim da Praça do Império**, before the late-Gothic Mosteiro dos Jerónimos **51** stops you in your tracks. After a tour of its magnificent cloister, treat yourself to a signature pastel de nata at Manteigaria **19**.

Length: 5.2 km
Walking time without stops: 1 hour, 10 mins
Start: Último Porto
**Not in guidebook*

N
48
*Praia da Santa Marta
*Palácio dos Condes
de Castro Guimarães
Cascais
AVENIDA MARECHAL CARMONA
AVENIDA MARGINAL
Monte Estoril
Estoril
66
*Praia da Poça
AVENIDA MARGINAL
67
500m
1km

3

WALK: THE PORTUGUESE RIVIERA

Culture-clad beach hop

Begin your coastal ramble at Casa das Histórias Paula Rego **48** in Cascais, one of the region's most striking works of architecture and home to an impressive collection by acclaimed Portuguese artist Paula Rego. Post gallery, head down to the lighthouse-marked waterfront, taking in *Praia da Santa Marta**, set next to the fairytale-like *Palácio dos Condes de Castro Guimarães**. Cling to the coastline, walking along Cascais's harbour, fortress and many beaches, all the way to lively Estoril. Just past the sandy bay, you'll find the ocean pool, Piscina Oceânica do Tamariz **66** – a nicely sheltered spot for a dip in the Atlantic. Dry off on the sand before your next leisurely beach hop. The route is a seafront promenade, with a smattering of *tascas* and bars looking over the coastline. Pass the beach of *Praia da Poca** before arriving at Praia da Azarujinha **67**, another grand mini-palace typical of this coast in tow. Lock in for some sunbathing in the little bay, fully in rhythm with the Lisbon beach-day spirit, before returning by train to the city.

Length: 5.1 km
Walking time without stops: 1 hour, 10 mins
Start: Casa das Histórias Paula Rego
**Not in guidebook*

N
250m
500m
750m
*Vino Vero
59
M Martim Moniz
*Miradouro
da Graça
*Arco Grande
de Cima
*Feira da Ladra
*Igreja de São
Vicente de Fora
54
Santa Apolónia
M
*Miradouro das
Portas do Sol
15
RUA DA MADALENA
*Museu do Aljube
*Miradouro de
Santa Luzía
*Sé de Lisboa
AVENIDA INFANTE DOM HENRIQUE

4

WALK: HISTORIC LISBON

Monuments and miradouros

Alfama is Lisbon's oldest neighbourhood: a Moorish quarter in medieval times, its name derives from the Arabic *al-ḥamma*, meaning 'springs' or 'fountains'. To tour its remarkable historic landmarks, start at Santa Apolónia Metro and begin the first ascent of the day through old Lisbon, the Panteão Nacional **54** rising from behind streets strewn with washing lines. If it's a Tuesday or a Saturday, don't miss the adjacent *Feira da Ladra** flea market, where you can haggle with vendors over eclectic finds. Continue your flaneuring, passing under the beautiful archway of the *Arco Grande de Cima** and alongside the Baroque church, *Igreja de São Vicente de Fora**. After more labyrinthine cobbled streets, pause for the views at *Miradouro das Portas do Sol** and the tiled *Miradouro de Santa Luzía**. Pass by *Sé de Lisboa**, Lisbon's cathedral, and the *Museu do Aljube**, a museum dedicated to the Portuguese fight against dictatorship. Stop for a bite at hyped *tasca* O Velho Eurico **15** before making one final climb to Jardim da Cerca da Graça **59**, nestled below the convent-topped *Miradouro da Graça**. Finish with a glass of wine at *Vino Vero**, set on one of Graça's most charming streets.

Length: 3 km
Walking time without stops: 50 minutes
Start: Santa Apolónia Metro
**Not in guidebook*

N
250m
500m
750m
*Jardim das Amoreiras
55
57
RUA DOM JOÃO V
M Ra
AVENIDA ÁLVARES CABRAL
RUA FERREIRA BORGES
8
RUA DE SÃO BENTO
*Centro Cultural
de Cabo Verde
58
50
CALÇADA DA ESTRELA
RUA DO POSSOLO
AVENIDA INFANTE SANTO
*Estufa
Dom Pedro V
*Jardim dos Cactos
60
30
T Santos
AVENIDA 24 DE JULHO
AVENIDA DE BRASÍLIA

5

WALK: GREEN POCKETS

Romantic park ramble

Start the day at neighbourhood cafe Tact **30** for speciality coffee and a fresh breakfast plate or a slice of baked cottage cheese, before striding on to the Romantic-era Tapada das Necessidades **60**. Trace its tangled pathways, passing the dusty-pink *Estufa Dom Pedro V**, crumbling regal structures and the *Jardim dos Cactos**, with sporadic views of the 25 de Abril Bridge through the foliage. Meander through the streets of Estrela, coming upon the ivory-white dome of the Basilica da Estrela **50**, before heading through the wrought iron gates of the Jardim da Estrela **58** just opposite. Take your time in this tropical pocket, looping its perimeter and grabbing a bica (espresso) at one of the kiosks, or lingering to read a book on the grass. Refuel with a hearty home-cooked lunch at By Milocas **8**, concealed in the *Centro Cultural de Cabo Verde**. For the final garden of the day, continue to the verdant *Jardim das Amoreiras**. Finally, for a dose of culture: you'll find the Baroque Águas Livres Aqueduct and Mãe d'Água Reservoir **57** here, alongside the quaint gallery Fundação Arpad Szenes – Vieira da Silva **55**.

Length: 4 km
Walking time without stops: 1 hour
Start: Tact
**Not in guidebook*

6

CANALHA

Welcoming neighbourhood bistro

Describing itself as Iberian but 'emotionally Portuguese', this highly respected local restaurant is deeply rooted in the country's culinary culture, from its elevated take on a classic interior to staple national dishes such as bitoque (steak topped with an egg) and pastéis de bacalhau (salt cod fritters) on the menu. The difference is that the produce at this Michelin Bib Gourmand eatery is of a uniquely high calibre, from the fresh fish counter to the cured meats hanging from the wall. Start with small plates such as lemon scallops and squid with sheep butter, followed by honest platters of grilled fish or meat paired with thick-cut chips and green salad. Weekday lunches offer fairly priced traditional soups and dishes of the day. Portuguese fare, done extremely well.

Rua da Junqueira 207, 1300–338
Nearest bus/tram stop: Altinho (MAAT)
(lines 201, 714, 727, 751, 15E)
paradigma.pt/venues/canalha

7
FAMILJEN

Creative global cooking

Sitting at the intersection of Portuguese seafood, Nordic cuisine and global flavours, this minimalist restaurant from Swedish chef Petter Nyström is an impressive display of creative cooking. With Lisbon's proximity to the ocean, you'll find plenty of fish on the short menu, innovatively prepared in the open kitchen: oysters with sea buckthorn and dill; raw yellowtail with lemongrass and cayenne pepper; suya octopus with cashew nuts and kimchi. The quality of the ingredients is evident in each dish (and you'll pay a premium for it) and the flavours drip with umami. The concise cocktail list is just as accomplished; don't miss the akvavit and dill 'Licence to Dill', a taste of the Nordics on ice. A hit among ardent foodies.

Rua do Machadinho 56, 1200–708
Nearest bus stop: Rua Esperança (Museu Marioneta)
(lines 706, 727, 774)
familjen.pt

First

Wilma's Spicy Margarita
Tequila, lime, agave,
jalapeno, piri piri   12

Licence to Dill
Jubileum Akvavit,
vermouth, lemon, dill   12

Oyster, sea buckthorn,
dill   3.5

Crispy Kale, raspberry
salt, smoked chill   6

Grilled Gordal Olives   4

Later

Yellowtail, lemongrass
& cayenne pepper sauce   16

Aubergine, miso,
roasted Sichuan pepper
vinaigrette   14

Green asparagus,
pistachio sauce,
wild roses   15

Turbot, nahm prik pao &   16
fresh herbs

Beef Tartare
roti, ho
grill

Later

8

BY MILOCAS

Joyful Cape Verdean cuisine

Buried in the basement of Lisbon's Centro Cultural de Cabo Verde (Europe's first African cultural centre), restaurant By Milocas serves up food from the island, a former Portuguese colony. Inside, it's light and airy, adorned with Cape Verdean artwork, figurines and clay pots. National dish Cachupa, a hearty stew served in steaming bowls, is a crowd choice, perfected by owner Milocas over the decades. Corn is a staple ingredient across the menu, from the pastéis de milho, sweet potato and corn pastries, to the mousse de camoca, a dessert made from roasted cornflour, condensed milk and cream. Find other Lusophone cuisine on the menu – all must-try dishes in the multicultural melting pot that is Lisbon.

Rua de São Bento 640, 1250–220
Nearest bus stops: Rua de São Bento, Rua do Arco
(lines 706, 727)
instagram.com/bymilocas

9

UAIPI

Cassava-centric Brazilian brunch

Couple Laila and Grégory are bringing the regional cuisine of Minas Gerais – a state in southern Brazil – to Lisbon with their little cafe, set in the backstreets of the Madragoa neighbourhood. From the decor to the cuisine, Uaipi is an ode to the traditions of the region's countryside. At the heart of the menu is nutty root vegetable cassava – 'the Queen of Brazil' – which shows up in myriad, highly moreish forms: fried with guava ketchup, freshly baked pão de queijo (cheese balls made with cassava flour), caramelised tapioca and coconut pudding. You can also take away homemade staples from their small grocery store: more of that tangy guava ketchup, tapioca granola and doce de leite – if you're lucky, the owners will give you a spoonful of this creamy caramel confection sprinkled with sea salt to send you on your way.

Travessa das Isabéis 18, 1200–689
Nearest bus stop: Rua Esperança (Museu Marioneta)
(lines 706, 727, 774)
instagram.com/uaipi.mandioca

URIPI
18
URIPI
BRAZILIAN
BREAKFAST
LUNCH
GLUTEN-FREE

10

ÚLTIMO PORTO

Grilled fish on the docks

During sardine season, little grills pop up all over the city to serve the masses. But for proper grilled-over-charcoal fish all year round, this lunch-only worker's joint in the Alcântara docks serves up the good stuff. It's set right between the container ships looking onto the River Tejo, with tables that catch the sun. The chef does mighty work with an A–Z of fish lining the griddle, golden and smoking. It comes the classic (and *only*) way: with boiled potatoes and vegetables and a wedge of lemon – a simple, salty, smoky plate that hits. The fish goes fast, so get here early or book a midday table to secure your first choice.

Rua General Gomes Araújo 1, 1350–352
Nearest train station: Alcântara-Mar
instagram.com/ultimoportorestaurante

11

TABERNA DA RUA DAS FLORES

Portuguese petiscos with a twist

Since its second day of business, this Portuguese tavern has ardently refused reservations. Instead, the hungry and determined should arrive early to jot their names down on an ever-growing list for a table. The frictious process, alongside the changing blackboard menu and the cash-only policy, is wonderfully old-school. Sometimes it pays off to work a little harder for your meal. While no longer housed in the rustic hole-in-the-wall two doors down (now the restaurant's bar), the quality of the dishes – and the service – remains steadfast. Classic, regional *petiscos* (small plates) are reimagined, often with an Asian twist, such as their signature scallops with miso butter; punchy corvina crudo with lime, chilli and coriander; and caramelised coconut prawns that steal the show.

Rua das Flores 109, 1200–194
Nearest metro: Baixa-Chiado
instagram.com/tabernadasflores

12

ZAYTOUNA

Unrivalled Palestinian mezze and wraps

Located in the north of the city, Arroios is one of Lisbon's most multicultural areas. Its domed market building, alive with early-morning traders, is also home to Zaytouna – a mecca for Middle Eastern fare. The colourful cafe–restaurant and grocery shop is stacked with jars of preserved lemons and makdous (cured aubergines stuffed with walnuts), tubs of tahini and sweet halawa, and bottles of pomegranate molasses and rose syrup. Those same goods are used in the small kitchen, serving up plates of mutabal (a creamier take on baba ganoush), hummus and tangy labneh cheese; pickle-laden falafel pittas; and cold glasses of rose lemonade for hot summer days.

Rua Ângela Pinto 19, Mercado de Arroios, 1900–221
Nearest metro: Alameda
instagram.com/zaytouna.pt

13
CAFEH TEHRAN

Persian bites on the square

Lisbon is an entire city of alfresco dining, but Cafeh Tehran stakes a claim to one of the finest outdoor spots. Little sun-dappled tables sit under colourful streamers on Praça das Flores, a rare-to-find homely spot in a bourgeois locale. Inside, it's like stepping into someone's living room, painted in vibrant blues and clad with Persian decor and photos. The menu is a medley of aromatic Iranian classics – ash reshteh soup, kookoo frittata, joojeh kebab, and the like – brought from owner Pooneh Niakian's motherland. Mix and match plates among friends and finish off with a spiced love cake or saffron ice cream on carrot and rosewater jam. Perfect for an afternoon lunch stop.

Praça das Flores 40, 1200–192
Nearest bus stop: Praça das Flores (lines 22B, 773)
instagram.com/tehrancafeh

14

LEONETTA

Elevated pasta fresca

Maximalism reigns supreme in this elegant pasta restaurant in Príncipe Real. The vintage Italian trattoria styling is impeccable, with framed posters and paintings covering every inch of wall, and jugs, plates and lamps peppering the shelves. Start with antipasti before moving on to a menu of pasta fresca supreme, made from scratch daily. Dishes range from the simple – mafaldine ribbons with stracciatella and tomato sauce; ricotta ravioli with spinach, butter and sage – to the extravagant – black pappardelle with lobster or paccheri tubes with guanciale, nduja and cured egg yolk. Indulgent plates and romantic, low-lit lighting make for a nostalgic dining experience – think *Lady and the Tramp*, with really good linguine.

Rua da Rosa 321, 1200–386
Nearest bus/tram stop: São Pedro de Alcântara
(lines 19B, 202, 758, 24E)
instagram.com/leonetta_lisboa

YOU CAN BE SURE OF SHELL
FIAT
CINZANO
COINTREAU

15

O VELHO EURICO

The buzziest tasca in town

You'll always find a queue on the sloping cobbled streets outside O Velho Eurico. It's an old *tasca* (a classic Portuguese restaurant) with a young spirit, taking hearty staples to the next level, from its famed bacalhau à brás (salted cod, potatoes and eggs) to sardine toast and tuna 'pica-pau' (in a garlicky gravy) – all scribbled on its blackboard menu. Mismatched tables, writing-covered tile walls and the joyous din of an always-full restaurant add to the riotous charm of the place. Energy reverberates off the walls as well-versed waiters dart back and forth with plates of squid and orange, duck rice and bread pudding – some of the best local food in the city. Book well in advance or take your chances with the queue.

Largo de São Cristóvão 3, 1100–179
Nearest metro: Rossio
instagram.com/ovelhoeurico

16
DURO DE MATAR

Tacos, radio and DJs

Doubling as a Mexican taqueria and a cultural venue, Duro de Matar is one of the most electric spots in Lisbon's vibrant Beato district. This former factory is now slick, silver and oozing cool, with muralled walls lit by neon strip lights, a pounding sound system and even a radio station in the back. It's always packed, an endless procession of smoky gringas, punchy tacos and zingy salsa leaving the kitchen, and lab-style beakers of margaritas, mezcals and Cristal beers flowing from the bar. As the night darkens, tables are cleared to make way for a dance floor. Don't come here if you can't dine amid din: it's a boisterous chorus of chatter, music and cocktail shaking, spelling a good night out.

Avenida Infante Dom Henrique 151, 1959–012
Nearest bus stop: Avenida Infante Dom Henrique
(Beato ID) (lines 728, 781, 782)
instagram.com/durodematar.pt

17
MERCADO DE CAMPO DE OURIQUE

Revived foodie market hall

Skip Time Out Market and head to this upscale local *mercado* instead, located in the centre of the classy Campo de Ourique neighbourhood. Under a swoop of arches, old meets new with a selection of typical produce stalls – baskets of plump fruit and vegetables, jars of dried fruits and nuts, artisanal pantry goods – alongside a smorgasbord of gourmet kitchens, serving everything from poke bowls to Middle Eastern fare, with a great oyster bar on hand. Grab a bite or a drink of choice and join the swathe of locals in the convivial dining area in the middle of the old market hall. A buzzy spot for solo diners and groups alike, often soundtracked by live music at weekends.

Rua Coelho da Rocha 104, 1350–075
Nearest bus/tram stop: Igreja do Santo Condestável
(lines 65B, 203, 709, 774, 25E, 28E)
instagram.com/mercadodecampodeourique

Carne
Meat Shop
Artisani
GELADO ARTESANAL
DEZEMBRO
NO MERCADO
natural. Feito todos os dias.

18
PATUÁ

Inside the foodways of Macau

This unassuming Macanese spot packs a punch with its fragrant curries and storied menu, dotted with tokens from chef Francisco de Jesus Rodrigues's family home. The name 'Patuá' refers to the patois language spoken in Macau, a former Portuguese colony, which blends Cantonese and Portuguese, with influences of Malay, Sinhalese and Indian languages. Macanese cuisine is a similarly rich fusion. Between dishes like 'Uncle Gégé's shrimp', cooked in a tangy Southeast Asian coconut broth, and spicy cafreal, the famous Mozambican dish that travelled to Macau via Goa, Patuá is a tale of both personal and collective history, tracing the movement of food cultures over five centuries.

Rua Angelina Vidal 71B, 1170–018
Nearest metro: Intendente
instagram.com/patua.lisboa

19

MANTEIGARIA

Unmatched pastéis de nata

Manteigaria might have a monopoly on the pastel de nata in Lisbon, but for good reason. These little pastry factories, dotted across the city, do one thing only, exceptionally well. With something of an assembly line going on within their glass-walled interiors, you can glimpse the team of pastry chefs crafting Portugal's famed custard tarts en masse. The chime of a bell punctuates each completed batch. At Manteigaria's marble countertops, sweet tooths in their scores dust still-warm pasteis with cinnamon and icing sugar. There's something extremely trustworthy – and nostalgic – about a business that's nailed a single offering.

Rua do Loreto 2, 1200–242
Nearest metro: Baixa-Chiado
manteigaria.com

MANTEIGARIA
Fábrica de Pastéis de Nata
AÇÚC
SUGA
SUCR
MANTEIGARIA
Fábrica de Pastéis de Nata

20

NANNARELLA

Gelato in a picturesque praça

Eating an ice cream on one of Lisbon's prettiest *praças* (squares) never ceases to be romantic – especially on mild winter days, sunlight filtering through the trees, when it's a small miracle to still be devouring gelato in December. Italian-owned Nannarella, a little ice cream parlour just off Praça das Flores, serves up the best, with queues stretching out of its door. The gelato is fresh and artisanal, with Italian classics, from nutty pistachio to creamy stracciatella, alongside Portuguese flavours, such as port wine and ginja (sour cherry). Craving something savoury? You'll find Rome-style pizza 'al taglio' (by the slice) from the same owner just next door.

Rua Nova da Piedade 64A ,1200–299
Nearest bus stop: Palácio de São Bento (Jardim)
(lines 706, 727, 773)
nannarella.pt

21

OSTERIA CUCINA DI AMICI

Comforting Italian cuisine

There's a charming chaos to this little *osteria*, a simple Italian eatery set on Santos's narrow backstreets. The mismatched Formica tables, red-and-white chequered napkins and Art Deco posters all spell the real deal. The kitschy cherry on top is the neon-flashing framed photo of the pope gazing down from high behind the bar – your blessing to have a good night. And with €6 negronis and limoncello spritzes that go down too easily, it's hard not to. Make your way through delicious, home-cooked plates of pizza frittas, meatballs in mamma's tomato sauce and tagliatelle with ragu. Leave tipsy and full-bellied.

Rua das Madres 52, 1200–712
Nearest bus stop: Rua Esperança (Museu Marioneta)
(lines 706, 727, 774)
instagram.com/osterialisboa

MERCEA
OSTERIA
VINHO
1A
Alarme
2017
2021
2024

22
O PALMEIRAL

Timeless all-day dining

O Palmeiral is a sigh of relief in a trend-driven restaurant landscape. Set in a 19th-century grocery shop, the antique glass cabinets today glisten with bottles of wine. It oozes old-school charm: tightly packed tables donned with white tablecloths and dripping dinner candles, along with original chequered floors and cream cafe curtains. The menu is built around perfected trattoria-style classics from owner Daniel Bernardi's Italian homeland, fused with Portuguese elements. Sample tortellini in brodo or roasted pumpkin with sheep's cheese, followed by aubergine parmigiana or their singular thick-cut pork chop. The kitchen is so small it doesn't even have a freezer – everything is fresh and sourced locally. And in the warmer months, eat alfresco on their sunny cornerside esplanada.

Travessa de São José 1, 1200–415
Nearest bus stop: Praça das Flores (lines 22B, 773)
opalmeiral.com

Palmeiral

23
MATUTA

Brazilian baked goods

Light, tangy and exceptionally moreish, pão de queijo is sure to be one of your best culinary discoveries in Lisbon. For the unacquainted, it's a classic Brazilian snack: a little ball of cheesy bread whipped up from tapioca flour. Neighbourhood cafe Matuta might just serve the best in the city. Making a name for herself with her cakes, Brazilian pastry chef and owner Eduarda Meireles works from passed-down family recipes, capturing the flavours of her region. The pão de queijo comes as is or stuffed – with mushroom, sausage, doce de leite and more – and the cakes in myriad forms – carrot cake with brigadeiro, ricotta cheesecake with guava, coconut cake and corn cake. Affordable, welcoming and baked to perfection.

Rua Actor Vale 15B, 1900–078
Nearest metro: Arroios
instagram.com/ma.tuta

24

CERVEJARIA RAMIRO

Riotous beer and seafood institution

This might just be Lisbon's most famous restaurant, reaching international stardom when Anthony Bourdain visited it to rave review on his show *No Reservations*. He described Ramiro as 'a barrage of minimalist seafood of maximum quality', a sentiment which still stands. Despite the hype, this place remains true to its origins, with locals and tourists alike facing the unavoidable nightly queue to get their fill of Atlantic offerings. Most make their way through a medley of sizzling prawns, garlic clams, stuffed crab and sea-salty goose barnacles, the cracking of crustaceans reverberating between the seascape-mural walls. If you're doing it right, 'dessert' here is a prego (a steak sandwich). Wash it all down with a steady onslaught of ice-cold beers.

Avenida Almirante Reis 1H, 1150–007
Nearest metro: Intendente
cervejariaramiro.com

SAGRES

25

GALETO

Late-night '60s snack bar

This iconic dining institution is the snack bar that doesn't sleep, serving the city daily from 7:30am to 3am. The colossal neon 'Galeto' sign has been lighting up the Avenida da República since the '60s, with a lore to match its years. It's something of an upscale diner, with a sizable labyrinth of varnished-wood bars and leather stools for bar-only dining. In a well-oiled operation, bow-tied waiters serve from their station behind the counter: pregos (garlic steak sandwiches) with fries or the signature 'Bife à Galeto' (an egg-topped steak with ham and pickles) landing atop the counters at an admirable pace. For something sweet, there are pancakes, waffles and a mountain of cakes behind the almighty dessert display. A true and unchanged Lisbon classic.

Avenida da República 14, 1050–191
Nearest metro: Saldanha

26

PRADO

Seasonal, sustainable plates and wine

Rooted in a farm-to-table philosophy, Prado is really a paean to quality, seasonal Portuguese ingredients. The name translates as 'meadow', with fitting connotations of abundance and fruitfulness. From melt-in-the-mouth smoked tuna belly to tender celeriac with hazelnuts and Judas's Ear fungus, single ingredients are elevated to new heights. Each plate looks like a little piece of art, painted with a Pollock-like splatter of emulsions and oils. The vegetarian dishes showcase the wonder of what a great chef can do with a vegetable, most exceptionally in the perfectly balanced mushroom ice cream with caramel and pearl barley. Next door, their wine bar offers local biodynamic and organic wines, alongside small plates that sing with the same creativity and quality.

Travessa das Pedras Negras 2, 1100–404
Nearest metros: Rossio, Terreiro do Paço
pradorestaurante.com

27

GARRINCHA

Creative Mediterranean cooking

Set in a former Portuguese *tasca*, with its tiled mural wall and silver bar, the understated setting and laid-back energy of Garrincha only draw more attention to the vivacious food. The chef cut his teeth in Paris's restaurants before opening his first venture in Lisbon, showing his culinary finesse in a daily-changing menu of Mediterranean dishes infused with flavours from the Middle East. Dishes are creative but understated, the fresh, quality ingredients shining through in each plate: sea bass caponata with tahini; cloud-light beetroot gnocchi; zingy kohlrabi salad; aerated chocolate mousse. And the wine is just as interesting – best enjoyed at the bar overlooking the buzz of the kitchen.

Calçada Poço dos Mouros 83, 1170–293
Nearest metro: Arroios
garrincha.restaurant

VILLA DE PONTE DE LIMA
1887

28

GUNPOWDER

Indo-Portuguese plates

With a large South Asian immigrant community, Lisbon has its share of curry houses, but at Gunpowder, you'll find high-end cuisine from the west coast of India that spices up local, seasonal produce and recipes. Dishes from the former Portuguese colony of Goa feature heavily, the two food cultures interwoven over 450 years of occupation. Take the French bean pakoras with chutney – a take on Portuguese green bean tempura; the tuna-fish croquettes – Portuguese-influenced snacks from Goa; or the seafood pulao – an Algarvian seafood rice in biryani spices – and the connection clarifies. Opt for a table downstairs in '70s-style decor, with a view of the open kitchen. Frying is the go-to technique here, so be sure to order a few of the zingier sharing dishes to balance out your plate.

Rua Nova da Trindade 13A, 1200–303
Nearest metro: Baixa-Chiado
gunpowderrestaurants.com/pt-lisbon

29

PASTELARIA VERSAILLES

Palatial pastry institution

One of a handful of historic Lisbon *pastelarias*, Versailles belongs to the tradition of the grand European cafe – once fashionable gathering places for politicians, socialites and intellectuals. Its interior is like stepping into a bygone era, with crystal chandeliers, ornate stucco ceilings, palatial mirrored walls and stained-glass windows. And all in the name of pastries. Today, Versailles is still bustling: locals on the go take their bica (espresso) at the counter, while bow-tied waiters serve hot chocolate to diners at tableclothed tables. Behind the long, marble-top counter is a mountain of baked goods to sample: sugar-dusted biscuits, cream-topped duchesses, sticky eclairs. Try the sweet, egg-based doces conventuais (convent sweets) for a historic pastry hit.

Avenida da República 15A, 1050–185
Nearest metro: Saldanha
grupoversailles.pt

30
TACT

Relaxed neighbourhood cafe

With its mid-century mosaic floor, marble walls and tall windows – fitted with Scandi-style wooden counter and tables – Tact is one of Lisbon's most aesthetic spots to enjoy breakfast. Vika and Kirill, the couple behind this honest, thoughtfully run cafe in Alcântara, pride themselves on the quality of their products: from fresh farmers' market goods to speciality coffee. The pair are as serious about coffee as their customers, rotating roasters and constantly sampling new notes, much to the delight of the regulars. Try their freshly roasted 'batch brew', accompanied by a slice of Slavic baked cottage cheese or yoghurt with granola, seasonal jam and dark chocolate. A reminder that simplicity done well goes a long way.

Rua Joaquim Casimiro 14A, 1200–697
Nearest bus stop: Avenida Infante Santo
(lines 713, 714, 727)
instagram.com/tact.cafe

31

VIDA DE TASCA

Long live the tasca

To really get to know Lisbon, look no further than the humble and unchanging *tasca*. These casual Portuguese eateries are the beating heart of the city: local spots for families and friends to gather over long lunches and dinners. No gimmicks, just reliable comfort fare: grilled fish with boiled potatoes and veg; one-pot seafood or duck rice; bitoque and the like. Enter Leonor Godinho to the *tasca* scene, a young Portuguese chef who abandoned fine and contemporary dining to try her hand at the traditional culinary lifestyle. Between the food and the atmosphere, her accordingly named Vida de Tasca (Tasca Life) has quickly become a city favourite. Get to know the *tasca* life – and all that it represents.

Rua Moniz Barreto 7, 1700–047
Nearest metro: Roma
instagram.com/vidadetasca

32
LERO LERO

Pizza, wine and music in style

Lisbon has its fair share of pizzerias, but the doubly chic and cool Lero Lero reigns supreme for pairing Neapolitan pizzas with biodynamic wine and stellar records. Plus, the Anjos local is known for dropping mixtapes, hosting slam poetry nights and throwing events spotlighting female and Black wine producers. The co-owners connected over their shared music taste, with records lining the shelves – funk, soul and disco leading the way – amid local bottles. Their eye for design is clear, with a polished mid-century interior: globe pendant lighting spilling out the hues of orange wine, Bauhaus and '60s Soviet lamps, and a curved bar centrepiece downstairs. In the warmer months, the vast windows are thrown open, filling the living room-like setting with a sweet summer breeze.

Rua Heliodoro Salgado 20A, 1170–177
Nearest bus/tram stop: Rua Forno do Tijolo
(lines 13B, 17B, 712, 726, 730, 734, 12E, 28E)
instagram.com/lero__lero___

STEREO
João Donato
sambou sambou
PACIFIC JAZZ
A PRODUCT OF LIBERTY RECORDS

33

A VIDA PORTUGUESA

Nostalgic Portuguese goods

Bordallo Pinheiro ceramic swallows, Couto toothpaste, Triunfo and Saloio olive oils: these are just a few of the storied products you'll find at old-school emporium A Vida Portuguesa, all hailing from long-standing, quality Portuguese makers. Containing everything from iconic packaging to tinsmithing and embroidery, the shop is a nostalgic archive of Portuguese craftsmanship, carrying memories of the past into the present-day home. It's also a love letter to the regional: tea from the Azores, shepherd's blankets from Alentejo, fleur de sel from the salt marshes of the Algarve. With multiple shops across Lisbon, A Vida Portuguesa is celebrated for giving Portuguese design a platform, showcasing generations-old brands alongside contemporary artisan talent.

Rua Nova do Almada 72, 1200–289, Chiado
Nearest metro: Baixa-Chiado
Other locations: multiple, see website
avidaportuguesa.com

34
UNDER THE COVER

Design-forward print

Shoebox-sized Under the Cover is (almost) single-handedly providing Lisbon with independent print. With a taste for provocative thinking and design, their fine-tuned curation of international magazines and coffee-table books spans arts, travel, food and beyond. While away the hours discovering a new indie publication or the latest edition from a familiar favourite, with everything from *The Gentlewoman* to *The Paris Review* and *Monocle* titles. Located just across the road from the Gulbenkian (no.46), take your new read to the gardens or combine it with an exhibition for a blissful afternoon of culture.

Rua Marquês Sá da Bandeira 88B, 1050–150
Nearest metro: São Sebastião
underthecover.pt

ARK JOURNAL

Wallpaper*
A GOLDEN AGE OF DESIGN

THE WORLD OF
INTERIORS

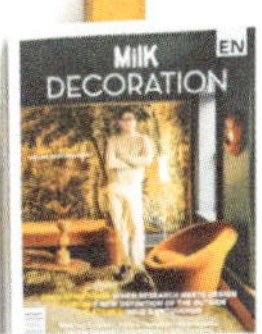
MilK
DECORATION
EN

RUM
HANDS ON

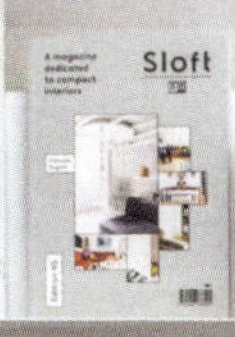
A magazine
dedicated
to compact
interiors
Sloft

THE NEW ERA
AGENDA

Openhouse

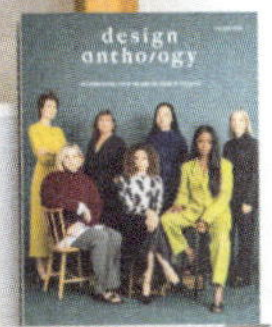
design
anthology

UPSTATE DIARY
DOWN TO THE ROOTS

91

apartamento

NEPTUNE

CABANA

We Are
Makers

By My Hands
A Potter's Apprenticeship
Florian Gadsby

bloom
gardening · nature · inspiration

rakesprogress

THE PLANT

sindroms

FAIRE

FAIRE

35

UNĀGI

Mecca for modern vintage fashion

Vintage fashion shops that aren't overwhelming are the best kind, and this minimalist little shop hits the bullseye – with reasonable price tags too. Unāgi is one of the few vintage fashion troves in Lisbon that consistently delivers the goods, thanks to the owner's impeccable curation and clear eye for standout pieces. The former fashion designer turned modern vintage connoisseur hand-picks every item from across Europe, with '90s and '00s garments dominating. It's a high-low mix, with designer names like Jacquemus and Prada among the selection, and a focus on long-lasting, quality garments. Keep an eye on their Instagram for their pop-up events with contemporary independent designers.

Calçada de Sant'Ana 88, 1150–306
Nearest metro: Martim Moniz
instagram.com/unagi.vintage

unāgı
68
90
MODERN VINTAGE

36

EMBAIXADA

Shop like royalty

You can find a surprising variety of experiences inside Lisbon's palaces: cinema screenings, hotel stays, DJ sets – or a concept store. EmbaiXada takes the 18th-century neo-Moorish Palácio Ribeiro da Cunha as its canvas for the latter, filling it with a curated selection of Portuguese brands, designers and artists. Browse Benedita Formosinho, with its merino wool and natural textile clothing, sister-owned swimwear and activewear brand Latitid, and the multi-generational family business Ecolã, producing wool products from the Serra da Estrela mountains. Frescoes, stucco ceilings and a stately staircase set the stage for a grand shopping affair, with a stunning central restaurant in the tiled internal courtyard.

Praça do Príncipe Real 26, 1250–184
Nearest bus/tram stop: Príncipe Real
(lines 202, 758, 773, 24E)
embaixadalx.pt

37
COMPANHIA PORTUGUEZA DO CHÁ

Multi-sensory tea haven

Created at the hands of an expertly trained tea sommelier, you'll find all manner of rare and fragrant blends from around the world in this sumptuous emporium: green Sichuan tea from Mount Meng Ding, smoked Lapsang infusions from the Azores, sweet honeybush from South Africa, Earl Grey made from bergamot harvested in Alentejo, chocolate-noted cocoa rooibos and Mao Jian from a small garden in China. Teas are stacked high across antique wooden shelves, in what was once a 19th-century shoemaker's shop. It's a feast for the eyes as well as the taste buds, with beautiful tins and packaging design. And after many brews, when all the leaves are used, tins become artful keepsakes to adorn mantelpieces.

Rua do Poço dos Negros 105, 1200–337
Nearest tram stop: Rua do Poço dos Negros (line 28E)
companhiaportuguezadocha.com

GABINETE

38
SALTED BOOKS

Expertly curated English-language bookshop

Awash in Egyptian blue from shelves to ceiling, Salted Books was the city's first English-language bookshop – and remains its most beloved. While other literary spaces have popped up in its wake, none can match the impeccable curation of the Santos independent, where experimental prose, cultural criticism and leftist non-fiction abound. With workshops, dedicated writing hours and literary talks, the space is as much a sanctuary for writers and the literary community as it is a shop. Never mind what drew you there, you'll be sure to walk away with a paper bag full of booksellers' recommendations, stamped with their slogan: 'Buy books from bookshops, not a billionaire.'

Calçada do Marquês de Abrantes 96, 1200–720
Nearest bus stop: Rua Esperança (Museu Marioneta)
(lines 706, 727, 774)
saltedbookslisbon.com

Buy books
from bookshops.
Not a billionaire.

39

KINTU STUDIO

Artist-crafted pieces

With its smattering of pottery studios, jewellery shops and galleries, Rua Poiais de São Bento is a stronghold for artists and artisans. At the light-filled Kintu Studio, you'll find a curated collection of handcrafted pieces from Portugal-and Brazil-based artists, designers and artisans. Across ceramics, illustration, jewellery, fashion and textiles, no two items are alike. From visiting artist studios to open calls, owner Sylwia Cylwik carefully sources statement pieces that carry the spirit of the creator in their form. As much as a store, it's a platform for these artists, with close to 80 represented here. Favourites include jewellery from Dassa Objects, Caution Fragile Ceramics and experimental objects by Pulp Studio.

Rua Poiais de São Bento 58, 1200–349
Nearest tram stop: Rua Poiais de São Bento (line 28E)
kintustudio.com

40
INÊS TELLES

Timeless artisanal jewellery

For locally crafted jewellery, look to Lisbon brand Inês Telles. Designed and sculpted at the hands of the namesake jeweller, silver and gold collections move between organic, asymmetrical and symbolic forms. Telles, a former art historian, learned her craft during an inspiring stint in Brazil, before returning to Portugal to launch her atelier. It's a small production focusing on traditional processes, giving the jewellery a distinctly handcrafted, tactile feel. Nature, curious cultural artefacts and places continue to inspire each collection. The light-filled little store opposite the Gulbenkian (no.46) offers a stylish place to browse the detailed pieces, spanning Inês' evolving collections.

Rua Marquês Sá da Bandeira 86C, 1050–150
Nearest metro: São Sebastião
inestelles.com

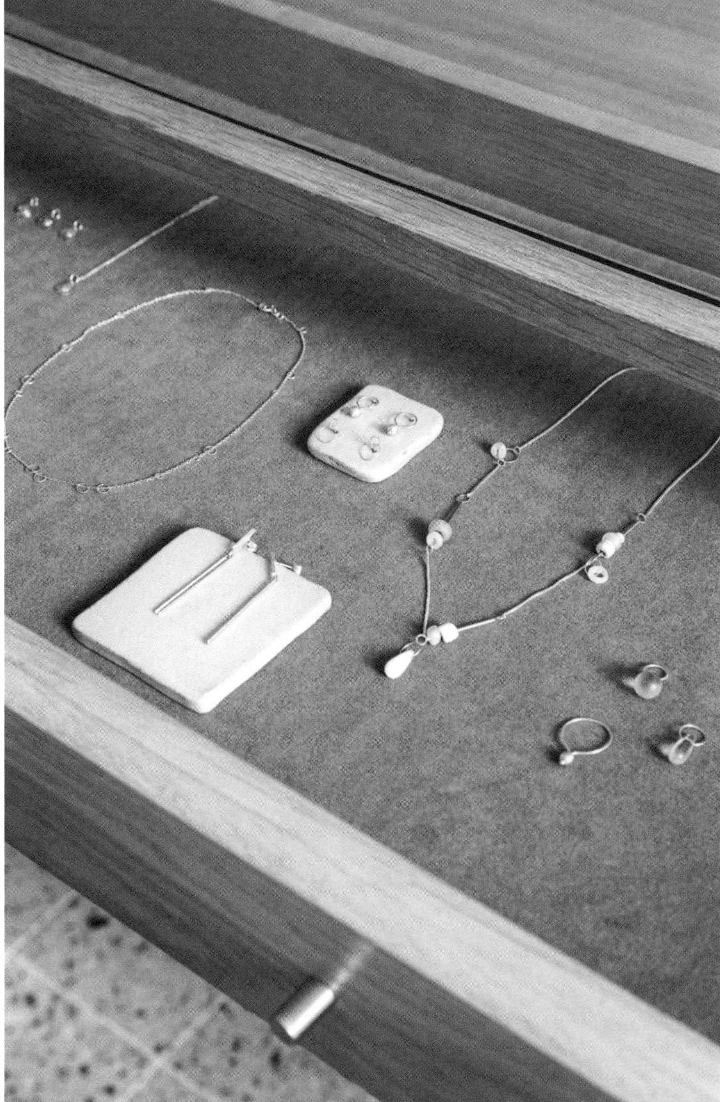

41
MANTEIGA CERÂMICA

Perfectly imperfect ceramics

Founded by Portuguese artist Marta Amador, ceramics studio Manteiga focuses on unique hand-built pieces, made sustainably. The name means 'butter' – mouldable like clay – and you'll find crafted butter dishes among fruit baskets, vases and jugs. Symmetry is rejected in favour of abstract shapes and rippling curves: a meeting of imperfection and perfection. Manteiga has an outpost on the volcanically formed island of Santa Maria in the Azores, and the red clay and natural tones of the land are integral to the studio's newer pieces. Head to the rustic Alcântara studio for a hand-building pottery workshop or to browse the ceramics.

Rua José Dias Coelho 4, 1300–328
Nearest tram stop: Calvário (lines 15E, 18E)
manteigaceramica.com

42
FAIRLY NORMAL

Surf-meets-city attire

Fairly Normal's distinct blend of coastal and urban culture sets it apart from your typical surf brand. Their classic-meets-contemporary pieces are designed to be seamlessly worn between shore and city, capturing the duality of lifestyles that makes Lisbon so unique. Surfer or not, relaxed cuts, sustainably-sourced fabrics and timeless styles make for long-lasting, high-quality capsule garments, all locally and responsibly produced in Portugal. Their flagship store is a slick white canvas for their minimalist apparel and surfboard collection, and hosts screenings and exhibitions on surf culture. It is conveniently located near the Cais do Sodré train station in case you want to drift over to the beach post-browse.

Rua de São Paulo 102, 1200–429
Nearest metro: Cais do Sodré
Other location: EmbaiXada
fairly-normal.com

FAIRLY NORMAL

43
GANDAIA

Novo Lisbon style

Describing their brand as 'good quality clothes for good times', Gandaia's colourful and relaxed-fit pieces carry the spirit of the contemporary Lisbon fashion scene. Formerly 'Mustique', the Lisbon-born indie brand has made an international splash with its unisex looks, quality pieces and vibrant prints. The 'made in Portugal' label is today a well-respected one, and Gandaia's production all happens nationally, with a commitment to natural textiles, quality craftsmanship and sustainability. Visit either of their stores in São Bento and Santos to browse their current collections and try out the effortless Lisbon look.

Rua Poiais de São Bento 90, 1200–377
Nearest tram stop: Rua Poiais de São Bento (line 28E)
Other location: Santos
gandaia.store

44
BRYON STUDIOS

Storied textiles and homeware

Bringing together a design studio, homeware shop and exhibition space, this is the creative project of designer Chloe Skinner – housed in a futuristic, light-flooded interior. Skinner defines her signature style as 'sentimental textiles', turning memories, imagination and motifs into whimsical screen-printed creations: clovers, marbles or treasures her children have found in nature. The focus is on small batches of hand-printed or hand-painted patterns on natural fabrics – including linens, silks and cottons. Napkins and tablecloths make for the most idyllic of summer picnics, alongside ceramics, rugs and tableware from fellow local artists.

Largo Vitorino Damásio 3C, Pavilhão 3, 1200–872
Nearest bus stop: Largo Vitorino Damásio
(lines 67B, 706, 727, 774)
bryonstudios.com

45

MAAT

Futuristic architecture on the water

On the banks of the River Tejo, the MAAT – Museum of Art, Architecture and Technology – is a curved shimmer of white geometric tiles. It's worth visiting for the building alone: walk along the sloped, overhanging roof of the low-slung structure, with views of the river stretching out to the ocean. Inside, spaces of varying shapes house rotating temporary exhibitions, while next door, the refurbished Central Tejo power station is an industrial canvas for more installations. To enjoy the riverfront pathway en route, walk or take a city bike from either Belém or Alcântara – it's one of the best places to move through the city (and completely flat).

Avenida Brasília, 1300–598
Nearest bus/tram stop: Altinho (MAAT)
(lines 714, 727, 15E)
maat.pt

46

FUNDAÇÃO CALOUSTE GULBENKIAN

Icon of Portuguese design

This sprawling cultural complex offers some of the best architecture and art in Lisbon. Its original 1960s modernist building – home to a world-class permanent collection and a concert hall – is designed into the landscaped gardens, where a concrete walkway loops through trees and bamboo groves. On the other side, find the recently redesigned Centro de Arte Moderna (CAM), with its sweeping Japanese-style canopy clad with hundreds of Portuguese tiles. It houses the largest collection of modern Portuguese art to date, including works by celebrated artists Paula Rego, Helena Almeida and Maria Helena Vieira da Silva, alongside temporary exhibitions. Don't miss a visit to the galleries on a Sunday, when entry is free after 2pm.

Avenida de Berna 45A, 1067–001
Nearest metro: São Sebastião
gulbenkian.pt

:

47

MUSEU DE ARTE CONTEMPORÂNEA

Portugal's largest cultural centre

A short stroll from the banks of the River Tejo, the Museum of Contemporary Art and Architecture (MAC), located within the Belém Cultural Centre (CCB), is one of Lisbon's most prominent cultural institutions. The permanent collection is a tour of modern art movements – from Cubism to Surrealism to Pop Art – with around 1,000 works by the likes of Picasso, Bacon, Dalí and many more legacy names on display. Its smaller temporary exhibitions are finely curated, offering a rotation of internationally renowned work. The fortress-like CCB was itself designed to be an 'open city', with internal squares, walkways and gardens to explore within the limestone-clad complex.

Praça do Império, 1449–003
Nearest bus/tram stop: Centro Cultural Belém
(lines 79B, 729, 15E)
ccb.pt/en/macccb

M
MAC/CCB
LISBOA
MUSEU DE ARTE CONTEMPORÂNEA
E CENTRO DE ARQUITETURA

48
CASA DAS HISTÓRIAS PAULA REGO

Earth-scorched emblem of Portuguese art

Slotted into the historic coastal town of Cascais, Casa das Histórias Paula Rego (Paula Rego House of Stories) is well worth the short train ride from Lisbon. The terracotta-hued pyramidal structure – a fiery blaze amid green lawns – is a striking architectural feat by Eduardo Souto de Moura, home to a collection of works by iconic Portuguese artist Paula Rego. The immersive archive of Rego's sketches, etchings and paintings draws deeply on folk and feminist subjects, displayed alongside pieces from her husband Victor Willing, the British painter. The gallery's temporary exhibition space features the works of contemporary artists in conversation with Rego, revealing the lasting effects of her radical work on the Portuguese art scene.

Avenida da República 300, 2750–475, Cascais
Nearest train station: Cascais

49

MUDE

A history of design and fashion

The newly renovated Museu do Design stands tall in a six-storey historic block right in the centre of Lisbon, an innovative incubator for all things architecture, furniture, fashion, print and beyond. Its permanent collection offers a comprehensive history of modern design, with everything from Christian Dior garments to Vespa's iconic scooter on display. In the basement, you'll find a striking exhibition space, with the building's former bank vaults now a canvas for temporary shows. Sustainability is a focus across MUDE's curation, with an emphasis on circularity and challenging the consumer economy. Don't miss the manicured rooftop terrace, with its unparalleled views of the Rua Augusta Arch.

Rua Augusta 24, 1100–053
Nearest metro: Terreiro do Paço
mude.pt

USEU
DESIGN
MUSE
MUDE
ENTRADA

50

BASÍLICA DA ESTRELA

Ivory basilica with rooftop walk

This pearly dome can be glimpsed from various points across Lisbon's hills, but it's best visited up close. While there are many worthy churches across the city, this one is atmospherically quiet, the Baroque-Neoclassical structure rising from the residential Estrela neighbourhood as yellow trams trundle past its doors. It's free to enter and beautiful inside, cast in grey and pink marble. For €5, ascend the winding spiral staircase and walk across the roof, gazing at the two bell towers and dome at scale against sweeping city views. Back on solid ground, head to the Jardim da Estrela (no.58) across the street for a final perspective of the magnificent monument.

Praça da Estrela 12, 1200–667
Nearest bus/tram stop: Estrela (Basílica)
(lines 713, 773, 774, 25E, 28E)

51
MOSTEIRO DOS JERÓNIMOS

Belém's late-Gothic marvel

It's worth braving the crowds to visit this UNESCO World Heritage Site, one of Lisbon's most famous historical monuments. The 16th-century Jerónimos Monastery took around 100 years to build, culminating in an ornamental masterpiece of late-Gothic Manueline architecture in historic Belém. The limestone cloister looks like it's spun from sugar, with opulent twisting pillars, shell-like turrets and maritime motifs in the stonework. In the adjacent ornate ivory-coloured church, you'll find the tombs of some of Portugal's most notable figures, including mariner Vasco da Gama, poet Luís de Camões and King Manuel I, who commissioned the monastery. Plan an early-morning or late-afternoon slot to avoid the hordes.

Praça do Império 1400–206
Nearest bus/tram stop: Mosteiro Jerónimos
(79B, 729, 15E)

52
PALÁCIO FRONTEIRA

Baroque palace and gardens

In the shadow of Parque Florestal de Monsanto (no.64) stands one of Lisbon's most beautiful – yet surprisingly lesser-known – palaces. Built in the 17th century, Palácio Fronteira was originally the hunting retreat of the first Marquis of Fronteira, whose family still call it home. Inside, tour grand rooms, historic *azulejos* (tiles) and the Arts Terrace, laden with marble statues of pagan gods. The Baroque gardens mesmerise with immaculate landscaping, a lake and the ornate blue and copper Gallery of Kings, with its busts of Portuguese kings past. Seek out the mystical grotto, elaborately decorated with a mosaic of smashed Chinese porcelain and shells. Time-weathered features add to the charm: moss-clad fountains, chipped tiles and peeling blue paintwork all whispering of a faded glory.

Largo São Domingos de Benfica 01, 1500–554
Nearest bus stop: Palácio Marquês Fronteira (line 770)
fronteira-alorna.pt/fronteira-palace

53
MUSEU NACIONAL DO AZULEJO

An odyssey through Portuguese tiles

Exploring Lisbon by way of its tiles is not a bad way to go, and at the Museu Nacional do Azulejo, you can see the very best of the treasured national art form. Housed in the 16th-century Convent of Madre de Deus, this museum is home to some of the country's most famous *azulejos* (traditional glazed tiles). Explore the evolution of the tile, from storied 15th-century pieces to more modern works, including those from the famed Portuguese sculptor Rafael Bordallo Pinheiro. The convent's church, clad in blue and white panels and gold wooden carving, is a lavish wonder to behold. Even the on-site cafe has a beautifully decorated interior, with fitting food-themed tiles and copper pots.

Rua Madre de Deus 4, 1900–312
Nearest bus stop: Igreja Madre Deus (Museu Azulejo)
(lines 203, 210, 718, 742, 759)
museunacionaldoazulejo.gov.pt

54

PANTEÃO NACIONAL

Lisbon's original Baroque monument

It took overcoming numerous hurdles to complete this domed Baroque monument in Santa Apolónia, including an incident of desecration and robbery, a curse from the falsely accused thief, and a colossal storm which saw the then-church crumble. This fractured history culminated in a 284-year process of completion – the longest of all of Portugal's monuments – christening an expression in its wake: '*obras de Santa Engrácia*', something without an end in sight. The result is a porcelain-white marvel, which evolved into the Panteão Nacional (National Pantheon) in 1916 and today holds the tombs of many of Portugal's greats. Up on the roof, find panoramic views of the old city against the River Tejo. If visiting on a Tuesday or Saturday, don't miss the adjacent flea market, Feira da Ladra.

Campo de Santa Clara, 1100–471
Nearest metro: Santa Apolónia
panteaonacional.gov.pt

55

FUNDAÇÃO ARPAD SZENES – VIEIRA DA SILVA

Modernist works from artist duo

Set in a former 18th-century silk factory, the light and airy galleries of this museum are dedicated to the works of Portuguese abstract painter Maria Helena Vieira da Silva and her husband, Hungarian expressionist Arpad Szenes. The collection is an emotive medley of texture and brushwork, with works by other like-minded artists also on display. At the forefront of the Art Informel movement, Vieira da Silva is renowned for her intricate geometric compositions of cityscapes and interiors, with the world's largest collection of her work found here. The charming on-site cafe offers a picturesque view over the tree-studded square beyond, beloved by the artist herself.

Praça das Amoreiras 56, 1250–020

Nearest metro: Rato

fasvs.pt

MUSEU ARPÁD SZENES VIEIRA DA SILVA

56

CINEMATECA PORTUGUESA

A technicolour world of vintage cinema

Just off Avenida da Liberdade, the glow of white neon lettering spells 'Cinemateca' atop a wrought iron gate. It's the entrance to a dreamy picture house, founded back in 1948, and dedicated to the preservation and dissemination of film heritage. Inside, it's a pocket world of retro cinema: film equipment and paraphernalia dot the interior, a cafe–restaurant is lined with vintage motion picture posters, and old movies have been playing daily since the '80s. Dig into its programme, explore its interior and exhibitions or muse over matters of culture with a drink on the terrace. A real cinema paradiso.

Rua Barata Salgueiro 39, 1269–059
Nearest metro: Avenida
cinemateca.pt

57

AQUEDUTO DAS ÁGUAS LIVRES

Grand aqueduct and temple of water

As you drive across the city, the arches of this great aqueduct appear unexpectedly, cutting dramatically across the landscape. It's a glimmer of old Lisbon – a grand Baroque structure that withstood the 1755 earthquake. You'll find its end by Jardim das Amoreiras, a swoop of arches flanked with tile murals, leading into the Mãe d'Água (Mother of Water) Reservoir. Step inside this under-visited temple, its design mirroring that of a church. Deep azure waters glisten and, where an altar would stand, a dolphin statue drips in moss and algae like something dragged up from the ocean depths. Soak in the serene, semi-spiritual mood of the place before climbing up to the cistern's roof for panoramic city views.

Praça das Amoreiras 10, 1250–020
Nearest metro: Rato

58

JARDIM DA ESTRELA

Tropical utopia by the Basilica

Thick with tropical plants, the green enclaves of Jardim da Estrela are a refreshing balm on Lisbon's hot summer days. Monkey puzzle trees, palms and cacti line the park's pathways, a banyan tree spreading its gnarled roots at the centre, statues and ponds hidden within. And with two kiosks, monthly weekend markets and DJ sets in summer, the park's charms are not limited to its nature. It's a constant hive of social activity: card games over coffee, children playing, friends picnicking on the grass. The chimes of the grand Basilica da Estrela (no.50), its dome visible through the tree-tops, punctuate the hours that quickly slip by here. Bring a book and settle in for the afternoon amongst the locals.

Praça da Estrela, 1200–667
Nearest bus stop: Jardim Estrela
(lines 713, 720, 738)

59

JARDIM DA CERCA DA GRAÇA

City park with historic views

This grassy hilltop park, folded in the wing of the Igreja da Graça, offers one of Lisbon's most scenic vistas of Castelo de São Jorge, a medieval Moorish castle and fortress. A butter yellow pergola adds to the charm, swimming in gold light come evening – a peaceful sundowner alternative to the Miradouro da Graça just above. By day, the park is a medley of picnickers, yogis, guitar-strummers and journal-carrying flaneurs, all out to soak up the carefree thrum of the place. A little kiosk keeps the gatherers refreshed – essential in the summer months.

Calçada do Monte, 1100–362
Nearest metro: Martim Moniz

60
TAPADA DAS NECESSIDADES

Walled royal gardens turned public park

Strolling through the 18th-century Tapada das Necessidades in Alcântara, once the royal family's private estate, you're met with a bygone grandeur somewhat typical of Portuguese gardens. Headless statues, peeling paintwork, a derelict dusty-pink domed *estufa* (greenhouse) and the former painting studio of Queen Amélia lie within – the weight of time and lost wealth tangible. Chickens wander amid enormous cactus groves, and sunbathers dot the grassy banks by the greenhouse in summer, the 25 de Abril Bridge visible above the palms and treetops. Despite its enduring beauty and history, this gloriously green spot remains quiet and tranquil all year round.

Calçada Necessidades, 1350
Nearest bus stop: Largo Necessidades (line 773)

61

JARDIM DO TOREL

Romantic garden with rooftop views

It's easy to miss the two-tiered Jardim do Torel, tucked away on a tranquil, tree-lined street of grand villas at the top of Santana Hill. Pass through its gates, however, and a portrait of Lisbon stretches out before you, all the way down to the River Tejo. This former estate garden was brought back to life in recent decades, designed around the concept of a 'garden of love'; fragrant lavender, verbena and pride of Madeira were planted and benches were restored, inscribed with poetry. The idea seems to have come to fruition, with couples cladding the grassy banks, sharing a bottle of wine as the sun sets behind city rooftops. A fountain graces the deck below, with open-air cinema screenings in summer.

Rua Júlio de Andrade, 1150–122
Nearest bus stop: Lavra – Rua Câmara Pestana (line 19B)

62

ESTUFA FRIA

Urban greenhouse complex

If you're not looking for Estufa Fria, you might not know it's there – partially buried in a former quarry on the slopes of the grand Parque Eduardo VII. This quasi-jungle is a sprawl of over 300 plant species, housed under a mammoth slatted canopy, walled by swooping concrete archways. Explore the main site – a colossal 'cold greenhouse' – via winding paths, with caves, ponds and mossy statues scattered among the dense greenery. The air is sweet, fresh and earthy. In Estufa Quente, the 'hot greenhouse', you'll find tropical vegetation, such as mango, coffee and banana trees, and in Estufa Doce, the 'sweet greenhouse', a tangled mass of cacti. Afterwards, stroll up the grand promenade, ending with a drink at Linha d'Água cafe.

Parque Eduardo VII, 1070–051
Nearest metro: Parque

63

JARDIM DO RIO

Riverbank park across the water

Gazing at Lisbon from the other side of the river is a bit like seeing a whole new city, the great canvas of the metropolis painted at all-new angles. Jardim do Rio (River Garden) is the ideal vantage point. Stretch out on grassy banks that kiss the water, the white sails of boats bobbing by. It's unmissable at sunset, the city cast in gold as the sun descends under the brick-red suspension bridge before you. To get here, cruise across the River Tejo on a ferry (leaving every 10–15 minutes from Cais do Sodré to Cacilhas) and walk along the jetty-strewed banks in Almada with their little river beaches all the way to the park.

Sítio do Olho de Boi, 2800–205 Almada
Nearest ferry terminal: Cacilhas

64

PARQUE FLORESTAL DE MONSANTO

Hiking trails in the city

This huge forested park is a vast tangle of tree-covered trails, panoramic viewpoints, hidden gardens and ancient ruins. Known as 'Lisbon's lungs', the sprawling expanse of nature offers a genuine escape from the city where, except for the occasional cyclist or runner, people are notably absent. Head to the Keil do Amaral Amphitheatre for its open grassy banks, dotted with sunbathers and picnic-goers, and soak in the view of the 25 de Abril Bridge and Cristo Rei monument rising dramatically out of the treetops. The adjacent Kiosk Keil do Amaral is the ideal spot to grab a Sagres beer and a tosta before getting happily lost again between the trees.

Estrada de Montes Claros, 1300–651 (for Amphitheatre)
Nearest bus stop: Cruz Oliveiras (lines 723, 724, 771)

65

PRAIA DE SÃO PEDRO DO ESTORIL

Easy beach getaway

With cliffs mottled with agave plants and waves awash with surfers, this sandy bay is a choice city escape. In the summer months, it's packed with punters, but that's all part of the spirit of a city beach. Pull out a towel and lock in for the afternoon, alternating between dips in the sea and cold drinks at the beachfront bar. At high tide, beachgoers scramble to move their clobber out of the ocean's path, while at low tide, green rock pools appear at the cliff's base – part of the coastline's protected ecosystem. Enjoy the day's last rays atop the craggy clifftop, the sky fading into pink, before slinking back to the city.

Praia de São Pedro do Estoril, 2765–529 Estoril
Nearest train station: São Pedro do Estoril

66
PISCINA OCEÂNICA DO TAMARIZ

Natural saltwater swimming pool

The rhythm of Lisbon days is often guided by the ocean, providing cool relief on hot days and reinvigorating dips throughout the year. One of the best places to swim near the city is Piscina Oceânica do Tamariz, a public saltwater pool protected from the choppy waves of the Atlantic by its stone walls, set at the end of Praia do Tamariz bay. Ladders and a stone slope offer routes into the chilly water amid seaweed-laden rocks and blue rock pools. Paddle out to one of the pool's platforms and watch the boats in Cascais harbour on the next bay over. To get here, take the scenic trainline towards Cascais, tumbling out just shy of the beach at the Riviera town of Estoril.

Praia do Tamariz, 2765–289 Estoril, Cascais
Nearest train station: Estoril

67

PRAIA DA AZARUJINHA

Picturesque beach on the Riviera

What this beach lacks in size, it makes up for in charm. Praia da Azarujinha is a vintage postcard of the Estoril-Cascais Riviera: a small sandy beach meets blue waters at the foot of towering stone walls, crowned with a turreted seaside villa and a neat row of palms. This area was once the summer playground of the aristocracy, with its whimsical, romantic villas and *palacetes* (small palaces) over-looking the ocean. Today, sheltered from the wind, it's a vibrant spot: clusters of sunbathers sprawl between sand, rocks and concrete, with chilled drinks in hand from the low-key beachfront bar. Stroll along the picturesque promenade all the way to Cascais, beach hopping at your leisure.

Praia da Azarujinha, 2765 Estoril
Nearest train station: São João do Estoril

68

FONTE DA TELHA

Laid-back beach living

You can almost hear the soft summer sound of 'The Girl from Ipanema' playing when you arrive at this relaxed Lisbon beach. It's a favourite spot on the vast Costa da Caparica, its beaches ever-wilder the further south you head, framed by fossil cliffs and sand-clogged forests. By the time you hit Fonte da Telha, you feel like you're somewhere else entirely – its wide sandy shore backing onto a tiny fishing village smattered with shacks lording beach paraphernalia. Linger at one of many beachside *tascas* for a long and languorous fresh fish lunch and a cold beer overlooking the ocean, salty, sandy and sun-kissed. The Caparica scenery and spirit are unparalleled.

Fonte da Telha, 2825 Costa da Caparica
Nearest bus stop: Fonte Telha (Praia)
(lines 3012, 3030, 3521, 3523)

69

PRAIA DA SAÚDE

Colourful fishing huts and sand dunes

Along with Fonte da Telha (no.68), Praia da Saúde, or 'Beach of Health', can be reached by taking a short drive across the 25 de Abril Bridge. While any beach on this sweeping coastline is a worthy choice, what sets this stretch apart is its smattering of colourfully striped wooden beach houses, lodged like oversized toys in the white sand. Now largely holiday homes, these were once the huts of fishermen – relics of the area's heritage. Today, you can still watch fishing boats bringing in their hauls right on the sand using a traditional technique called *Arte-Xávega*. Sample the day's catch at one of the coastline's many eateries – Restaurante Praia do Rei is a favourite spot for dining with your toes in the sand.

Praia da Saúde, Costa da Caparica, 2825
Nearest bus stop: Estr F Telha (X) Praia Saúde
(lines 3030, 3044)

70

PRAIA DO GUINCHO

Rugged beach at the edge of Europe

Nearing Europe's most western point, this sandy beach is set against the mist-clad Sintra Mountains in a haze of gold and green. As part of the Serra de Sintra national park, Guincho oozes the raw and wild force of nature, with winds famed for blowing a mighty gale here, making it a fierce spot for surfing and kitesurfing. Explore the unspoilt landscape further with hiking trails winding into the mountains or wooden walkways spidering across the inland dune system. The beach is best reached atop a city bike from Cascais, following the 9-kilometre cycle lane as it snakes alongside the rocky coastline, wind whipping in your hair. It doesn't get much better than this.

Praia do Guincho, 2750–642, Cascais
Nearest bus stop: Praia do Guincho (lines 5, 43)

71
SANTA CLARA 1728

Slow living in the city

Beginning as a family beach home that proved a hit in the design world, Silent Living has since expanded to five hotels across Portugal. Six-bedroom Santa Clara 1728 is housed in a former monastery, its preserved arches, staircases and stonework steeped in memory. Thoughtful design features abound throughout the intimate hotel, soft tones and materials bleeding seamlessly into the Panteão Nacional (no.54) just across the way, with upstairs views of its dome set against the River Tejo. The 6-metre oak table is the setting for nourishing breakfasts and the site of farm-to-table lunch restaurant Solo and dining experience Ceia, with all produce sourced from the owners' regenerative farming project in Alentejo. It's the kind of space that commands real presence, leaving you reeling at the sight of an iPhone.

Campo de Santa Clara 128, 1100–473
Nearest bus stop: Mercado de Santa Clara (lines 734, 797)
silentliving.pt/houses/santa-clara-1728

72

PÁTIO DO TIJOLO

Design-led courtyard hotel

You'd be hard-pressed to imagine that a spacious, modern hotel exists in the tight-webbed cobbled streets between Bairro Alto and Príncipe Real, but here Pátio do Tijolo is, tropical garden and all. Design is in the bones of this place, from the modernist shell down to the contemporary furniture and artwork. Across its floors, you'll find three spaces to make yourself at home in: a swish kitchen and dining room, a light-flooded library and a verdant greenhouse–living room hybrid – each as immaculately styled as the next. Bold shapes and hints of the industrial proliferate – a wash of neutral palettes with splashes of colour. Downstairs, the leafy courtyard is a manicured urban oasis, from which the city feels far away.

Calçada do Tijolo 41A, 1200–464
Nearest bus stop: Rua da Rosa / Travessa de São Pedro
(line 22B)
patiodotijolo.com

73

HOTEL DAS AMOREIRAS

Country-luxe house on the square

There's a country house feel to this boutique hotel, a luxurious double townhouse on one of Lisbon's most charming squares (and one of the city's best-kept secrets). Owner Pedro Oliveira took inspiration from the grand hotels of Europe, British interior design and the homes of designers like Ralph Lauren and Yves Saint Laurent, meaning everything here has a classic, luxury feel. Plush fireside armchairs, a '70s upholstered bar, grass-cloth wallpaper and paintings from the owner's collection all add to the heritage maximalist aesthetic. Take a made-to-order breakfast in the quaint courtyard garden or enjoy afternoon tea in the cosy lounge. You'll find the best suites on the top floor, overlooking the leafy Praça das Amoreiras and Águas Livres Aqueduct (no.57).

Praça das Amoreiras 34, 1250–020

Nearest metro: Rato

hoteldasamoreiras.com

74

LOCKE DE SANTA JOANA

Convent turned elegant hotel

From the high-end Portuguese brasserie helmed by Nuno Mendes, one of the country's most celebrated chefs, to the underground listening bar The Kissaten, via sun-kissed lunch spot Santa Marta, and Bond-esque cocktail bar Sacra – there's little left to be desired at this chic city resort, complete with upscale central pool and sunloungers. But despite the behemoth scale of the place, the beauty of Santa Joana is in the details. The main building and restaurant are in the reimagined old convent, with preserved archaeological details throughout the hotel, from 17th-century tiles to ancient urinals. There's even a small museum of some of the 20,000 Roman and Neolithic artefacts found here during the excavation. Historic surrounds, contemporary lifestyle.

Rua Camilo Castelo Branco 18, 1150–084
Nearest metro: Marquês de Pombal
lockeliving.com/en/lisbon/locke-de-santa-joana

75

A VIAGEM DAS HORAS

Vinyl-led wine bar

An unpretentious natural wine bar is something of an oxymoron, but this relaxed local favourite pulls it off. Records line the walls of the snug Arroios spot: Roy Ayers, Sade, Prince, Nina Simone, with the titular album *A Viagem das Horas* from Brazilian artist José Mauro front and centre. The name translates to 'the journey of the hours', and the hours here slip away to the rhythms of jazz, soul and funk over a glass of something equally funky. Music is integral, thanks to Angolan owner Ricardo Maneira, best known as DJ Rykardo, whose vinyl collection is second to none. Linger on the terrace on summer evenings, sipping low-intervention wine, sampling their 'playlist' of small plates or checking out one of their diverse kitchen pop-ups.

Rua José Ricardo 1, 1900–285
Nearest metro: Arroios
instagram.com/aviagemdashoras

a viagem das horas
a viagem das horas
BEIJA FLOR
SOUND SYSTEM
HORÁRIO
TER-SÁB
17H-00H

76

QUIOSQUE DO PIPO

Coolest kiosk in town

Dotted throughout every district in Lisbon, kiosks offer the kind of third spaces most cities are sorely lacking in. New-on-the-block Quiosque do Pipo – so named after the owners' beloved sheepdog, who frequents the hangout most nights – have knocked it out of the park with their laid-back vibes and excellent tunes. From their little kitchen, they serve up delicious, messy bites such as dirty fries and cheese steak or mushroom sandwiches, which require a wad of napkins and always hit the spot. Also on offer are unmatched tequeños (Venezuelan cheese-dough sticks) and yucca fries. These signature snacks, washed down with spicy margaritas and hard-to-come-by Guinness, have gained them a cult following, with faithfuls flocking for their weekly fix.

Largo Santos, 1200–808
Nearest bus stop: Largo Vitorino Damásio
(lines 67B, 706, 727, 774)
instagram.com/quiosquedopipo

QUIOSQUE DO PIPO
GUINNESS

77

INSACIÁVEL

Rustic natural wine bar with small plates

Nothing feels more European than sipping a glass of local wine outside on a warm summer's night, and neighbourhood bar Insaciável is pure romanticism. Bulb lights are strung from trees, criss-crossing tables and chairs perched on a cobbled Santos street. Attentive apron-wearing sommeliers bring out bottles for sampling, with a focus on natural wines from small-scale Portuguese producers. *Pratinhos* (small plates) are also on offer, such as chimichurri potatoes, corvina ceviche and mixed local cheeses – all served on mismatched patterned plates. Inside, the old piano, vintage fixtures and wine cellar add to the rustic feel.

Rua da Esperança 156, 1200–660
Nearest bus stop: Rua Esperança (Museu Marioneta)
(lines 706, 727, 774)
instagram.com/insaciavel.lisboa

78

MIRADOURO DE BAIXO

Understated rooftop bar

A Lisbon rooftop is an important touchpoint, but skip the high saturation of flashy panoramic bars and hotel terraces and opt for this more laid-back spot instead. Just beyond the large central square of Martim Moniz, the wide-open rooftop of Miradouro de Baixo sits atop the cultural centre Carpintarias de São Lázaro, graced with superior views that peer up at the Moorish castle and Graça's convent. Stop by during the early evening, savouring the hour when the scattered layers of the city's buildings are baked in gold. For a DJ set or live music overlooking the skyline, often with enticing kitchen pop-ups, explore the venue's eclectic cultural programming.

Rua de São Lázaro 72, 1150–330
Nearest metro: Martim Moniz
instagram.com/miradourodebaixo

79

MIRADOURO DO MONTE AGUDO

Secret sunset spot

Lisbon's many *miradouros* (viewpoints) offer some of the best gathering spots in the city, where catching the sunset is something of a social occasion. Hidden in the trendy Anjos neighbourhood up an unassuming set of steps, you'll find tree-topped Monte Agudo – the locals' viewpoint. The tourist throngs are notably absent; instead, it's a young, laid-back crowd, meeting friends between the graffiti-scribbled old pavilion and Simo's kiosk. The latter serves the crowds with first-rate cocktails, tostas and music; snag one of its deckchairs and watch the sun go down over the pastel city. Golden hour here never gets old.

Rua Heliodoro Salgado, 1170–175
Nearest metro: Anjos

80

AMOR RECORDS

Happening record shop and listening bar

Come the week's end, you'll always find a crowd spilling onto the cobbled streets outside bar-slash-record-shop Amor Records. Inside, crates of vinyl line the walls – Brazilian beats alongside a diverse selection of funk, soul, house and jazz – and live DJs set the mood. Founded by Thiago Guiselini, father of Soul Set in São Paulo, Amor has gained a solid reputation within Lisbon's music scene, known for its curated electronic events across the city. The space itself is an intimate, living room-type affair, lit in Dionysian red, with drinks sipped between the records. A great place to start the night before heading to the next spot in Anjos – often with the eclectic group you've gathered there.

Rua Frei Francisco Foreiro 2A, 1150–166
Nearest metro: Anjos
instagram.com/records.amor

amor records

81

A PARÓDIA

Cocktail bar with a past

Ring the bell outside A Paródia and step into a kaleidoscope of vintage Bohemia – all chintzy lamps, stained glass and snug booths upholstered in plush velvet. This was originally the antique shop of famed collector and designer Luís Pinto Coelho, and a gathering place for supporters of the 1974 revolution. Just two days after the fact, it officially opened as a bar and hotbed for artists, politicians and writers. History runs through the veins of this place, its name referencing the iconic satirical Portuguese magazine, with framed copies splayed across its wood-panelled walls. Across the city, you'll find three more of Coelho's legendary bars: Procópio, Foxtrot and Pavilhão Chinês – all decadent pocket worlds of the past.

Rua do Patrocinio 26B, 1350–229
Nearest bus/tram stop: Rua Saraiva de Carvalho
(lines 65B, 203, 709, 774, 25E, 28E)
aparodia.com

82

TEJO BAR

Legendary musicians' haunt

This tiny but legendary bar is a gathering place for locals and musicians, with icons such as Madonna among its patrons. Offering an alternative take on the classic *fado* houses of the area, its sounds are diverse and experimental, with Cape Verdean morna and Brazilian bossa nova alongside the famous Portuguese folk music. The walls are decked with instruments and an improv spirit abounds – you never know who might join in, be it a drinker from amid the crowd or someone from behind the bar. With no talking, no photos during performances and hands rubbed together in lieu of clapping, it's an intimate and immersive musical experience. Arrive early to knock on the door and grab a stool, with €5 entry going towards the artists.

Beco do Vigário 1A, 1100–613
Nearest bus stop: Rua Dos Remédios
(lines 10B, 13B, 734)
instagram.com/tejobar.oficial

DRAMA BAR

Queer bar and hub for local culture

'These gays, they're trying to murder me', reads one of the posters plastered on the walls of Drama Bar. Drama is in the name, and you're sure to find it in the theatrical programming and campy paraphernalia of this cool Anjos hotspot. It's a queer space, in the true and broad sense of the word, founded by couple Damien and Gauthier to offer an inclusive gathering place for marginalised groups. The main bar, with its DIY mix of tableware and knick-knacks, is a welcoming spot for sipping a cocktail under charged red lights, while downstairs you'll discover their event space. Friday and Saturday nights focus on music, while Sundays are for drag and cabaret shows. An Anjos neighbourhood staple.

Rua Damasceno Monteiro 75B, 1170–113
Nearest metro: Intendente
instagram.com/dramabar.lisboa

84

FÁBRICA BRAÇO DE PRATA

Arms factory turned cultural centre

Once a dilapidated arms factory from the days of Portugal's dictatorship, this complex was transformed into a vibrant cultural centre back in 2007, retaining its name, which translates as 'Silver Arm Factory'. The project was a major milestone in Lisbon's cultural evolution and the development of Marvila into a thriving post-industrial district – now the city's coolest nightlife area. The sprawling arts association is a maze of rooms overflowing with books, walls splashed with colour and murals, concert spaces and bars. Check out their schedule of music, dance, cinema and talks to see what's happening on any given weeknight or weekend. With galleries, pop-ups and craft breweries, this happening waterfront locale is well worth the ride east.

Rua da Fábrica do Material de Guerra 1, 1950–128
Nearest bus stop: Poço Bispo
(lines 210, 718, 728, 755, 781)
fabricabracodeprata.com

85

GALERIA ZÉ DOS BOIS

Cult music and arts venue

Cultural associations are the backbone of Lisbon's nightlife, and Galeria Zé Dos Bois is a classic. Founded back in the '90s, this non-profit is a passionate supporter of the arts with its diverse programme of experimental music, theatre, dance and visual arts. The multi-floor venue – combining gallery, events space, bookshop and bar – is a cult evening spot to grab drinks or catch a gig in low-key, alternative surrounds. You'll find most of the crowd on the terrace, sheltered from the throng of the Bairro Alto neighbourhood. Check what's on in advance and remember to bring cash, as cards aren't accepted.

Rua da Barroca 59, 1200–047
Nearest metro: Baixa-Chiado
zedosbois.org

IMAGE CREDITS

Page 2 © Mircea Solomiea; page 4 © Róza Kadi; page 6 © Manuel Gomes da Costa; page 7 © TaitG / Adobe Stock; page 8 © Joana Freitas; page 9 © Dmitry Rukhlenko / Adobe Stock; Canalha © Joana Freitas; Familjen © Émilie Hamon; By Milocas © Austin Bush / Culinary Backstreets; Uaipi © João Azevedo; Último Porto © Nic Crilly Hargrave; Taberna da Rua das Flores © Hayley Kelsing; Zaytouna © choicofmagic.com; Cafeh Tehran © Shab Ahanin; Leonetta © Issy Croker; O Velho Eurico © Luís Miguel; Duro de Matar © Cris Costa; Mercado de Campo de Ourique © Alexandre Rotenberg / Alamy; Patuá © Adriana García Lorenzo; Manteigaria © Manteigaria; Nannarella © @NatachaEats; Osteria Cucina di Amici © Teresa Lopes Gregório; O Palmeiral © Sebastião Santos; Matuta © Claudia Regina Pereira; Cervejaria Ramiro © Heather Steele; Galeto © Rodrigo Simões Cardoso; Prado first image © Rodrigo Simões Cardoso, second image © Joana Freitas, third image © Rodrigo Simões Cardoso; Garrincha © Manuel Manso; Gunpowder © Antonio Camacho; Pastelaria Versailles © Stefano Politi Markovina / Alamy Stock; Tact © Manannikova Nadezhda; Vida de Tasca © Inês Matos Andrade; Lero Lero © Violena Ampudia; A Vida Portuguesa © Pedro Sadio / A Vida Portuguesa; Under the Cover © Fabio Carvalho; Unāgi © Unāgi; EmbaiXada © EmbaiXada; Companhia Portugueza do Chá © Charlotte Valade; Salted Books © Teresa Brás; Kintu Studio © Kintu Studio; Inês Telles © Sanda Vuckovic; Manteiga Cerâmica © Manteiga Cerâmica; Fairly Normal © Sebastian Kamilaris; Gandaia © Luísa Bravo; Bryon Studios © Tanya Yarmolovych; MAAT © Francisco Nogueira; Fundação Calouste Gulbenkian © Fernando Guerra; Museu de Arte Contemporânea © Rita Carmo; Casa das Histórias Paula Rego © View Pictures / Getty; MUDE © Luisa Ferreira; Basílica da Estrela © Amazing Aerial / Alamy Stock Photo; Mosteiro dos Jerónimos © Vitor Ribeiro / Adobe Stock; Palácio Fronteira © Jon Arnold Images Ltd / Alamy; Museu Nacional do Azulejo © Picturelibrary / Alamy; Panteão Nacional © Cephas Picture Library / Alamy; Fundação Arpad Szenes – Vieira da Silva © Vasco Celio; Cinemateca Portuguesa © Jeffrey Isaac Greenberg / Alamy; Aqueduto das Águas Livres © Ian Pilbeam / Alamy; Jardim da Estrela © Adobe Stock; Jardim da Cerca da Graça © Carla Guedes Pinto / Alamy; Tapada das Necessidades © Adobe Stock; Jardim do Torel © Uma Brasileira; Estufa Fria © Mauro Rodrigues; Jardim do Rio © Alberto Seabra; Parque Florestal de Monsanto © Adobe Stock; Praia de São Pedro do Estoril © Mariya Bozhkova / Alamy; Piscina Oceânica do Tamariz © Aneymannv Media; Praia da Azarujinha © Gabriel Mello / Getty Images; Fonte da Telha © Mauricio Abreu / Alamy; Praia da Saúde © Adérito Valentim; Praia do Guincho © Connect Images / Alamy; Santa Clara 1728 © Richard Gaston; Pátio do Tijolo © Manuel Gomes da Costa; Hotel das Amoreiras © Francisco Nogueira; Locke de Santa Joana © Francisco Nogueira; A Viagem das Horas © V. Sheree Williams; Quiosque do Pipo © Isabella Kosaniuk and Oriol Acevedo; Insaciável © Róza Kadi; Miradouro de Baixo © Miradouro de Baixo; Miradouro do Monte Agudo © Olga Shatokha; Amor Records © Amor Records; A Paródia © Jussi Puikkonen / Alamy; Tejo Bar © Andrei Antipov / Alamy; Drama Bar © Image featuring @ Marge_Mellow, courtesy of the artist; Fábrica Braço de Prata © Mariana Lefeber; Galeria Zé dos Bois © Beatriz Pequeno.

An Opinionated Guide to Lisbon
First edition, first printing

Published in 2026 by Hoxton Mini Press, London.
Copyright © Hoxton Mini Press 2026. All rights reserved.
Text © Ruby Conway 2026.

Text by Ruby Conway
Editing by Kate Overy
Production design by Dom Grant
Production control by David Brimble
Proofreading by Dean Drake
Editorial support by Emma Seckel and
    Olivia Kumar

With thanks to Matthew Young for
initial series design.

Please note: we recommend checking the
websites listed for each entry before you
visit for the latest information on price,
opening times and pre-booking
requirements.

The right of Ruby Conway to be identified
as the author of the text has been asserted
under the Copyright, Designs and Patents
Act 1988.

Thank you to all of the individuals and
institutions who have provided images
and arranged permissions. While every
effort has been made to trace the present
copyright holders we apologise in advance
for any unintentional omission or error,
and would be pleased to insert the
appropriate acknowledgement in any
subsequent edition.

No part of this publication may be
reproduced, stored in a retrieval system,
or transmitted in any form or by any
means, electronic, mechanical,
photocopying, recording or otherwise,
without the prior written permission of
the copyright owner.

A CIP catalogue record for this book is
available from the British Library.

ISBN: 978-1-917719-21-6

Printed and bound by OZGraf, Poland

Manufacturer: Hoxton Mini Press, 104
Northside Studios, 16–29 Andrews Road,
London E8 4QF, UK
www.hoxtonminipress.com

Represented by: Authorised Rep
Compliance Ltd., Ground Floor, 71 Lower
Baggot Street, Dublin DO2 P593, Ireland
www.arccompliance.com

Hoxton Mini Press is an environmen-
tally conscious publisher, committed
to offsetting our carbon footprint.
This book is 100 per cent carbon
compensated, with offset purchased
from Stand For Trees.

Every time you order from our website, we
plant a tree: www.hoxtonminipress.com

Selected opinionated guides in the series:
For more go to www.hoxtonminipress.com

ABOUT HOXTON MINI PRESS

Hoxton Mini Press is a small indie publisher based in east London. We make beautiful books with a dedication to sustainable production and great photography.

When we started the company, people told us print was dead; we wanted to prove them wrong. Books are no longer just about information, but objects to collect and own.

We promise three things. Firstly, nothing in this guidebook is sponsored; it's our own independent opinion. Secondly, our books are 100 per cent carbon compensated with printing, paper and transport fully offset. And finally, everything is researched, edited and written by humans, not AI.

INDEX